START YOUR ZERO WASTE HOME

HOW TO SAVE MONEY, SAVE THE ENVIRONMENT AND SIMPLIFY YOUR LIFE BY LEARNING TO REUSE, RECYCLE AND REDUCE YOUR WASTE

NICOLE MENENDEZ

CONTENTS

Acknowledgments   i

INTRODUCTION   1

1   EAT MORE, THROW LESS: NO WASTE KITCHEN   3

2   REUSE, RECYCLE: NO MORE PLASTIC PACKAGING   12

3   SAY NO TO DISPOSABLE PRODUCTS (OR REUSE THEM)   18

4   FIX EVERYTHING (OR HAVE SOMEONE ELSE DO IT)   23

5   GROW VEGETABLES AT HOME   26

6   LESS IS MORE: BUY LESS AND BE MORE   31

ACKNOWLEDGMENTS

First of all thank you to my big brother Marc for encouraging me to embark upon this project and making anything seem possible. Also for teaching me the technical stuff and helping me in every step of the production process. Thank you to my husband Kristoffer for the countless hours of keeping the children busy while I write. Thank you to my editor Chris Rasmus and to Tropical Publishing Group for making this book possible.

INTRODUCTION

We live in a world with a one-way system. We take resources, use them and bin them. Most waste ends up in landfill sites. The problems with landfill are many. Materials like plastics and metals take many hundreds of years to break down, if they do at all. This means that we accumulate rubbish at an exponential rate, especially since the population is still on the increase. Toxins from the waste products are released over time into the soil and end up in our water supply and in our food. Organic waste becomes robbed of oxygen as the layers of landfill cover it, leading to a huge build-up of methane, the most terrible of the greenhouse gases. A lot of plastic waste ends up being broken down into tiny particles which pollute our seas and are ingested by fish, which we then eat. Many of these particles will never disappear.

What is the solution to this well-known problem? YOU are. You have the power to change the course of our species and slow it all down. All you need to do is learn a little and apply the knowledge in order to change a few habits and reduce your household waste. There are many ways to reduce and eliminate waste. In this book you will find tons of ideas and ways to reduce your waste and to reduce your consumption thereby starting your zero waste home.

I would like to tell you a little bit about a small and innovative country that I've had the pleasure to live in and learn from. Its name is Sweden. I landed there on the 6th of January 2009. I drove for 7 hours to my final destination, a little village by the name of Funäsdalen. When I climbed out of the car, my nostrils stuck together from the cold. It was -35°C (-31°F). I was a little shocked, having grown up in Spain and the UK. To my surprise I learned to love the place and the people of the town welcomed me with open arms. Eventually I even learned to tell the temperature through my nose! Sweden is a pioneer in sustainable waste management. During the 10 years that I lived there, Sweden reduced its landfill waste to less than 1% of the total waste generated in the country. That is simply amazing. I take my hat off to you Swedes. You are my inspiration for this book. Sweden changed my attitude from the learned helplessness that I had been indoctrinated in (what's the freakin' point it's all everybody else's fault and big industry controls everything) to an empowered, energetic and proactive approach. I can do this, I have changed and it was not impossible.

WHAT YOU GET

In this book you will find out:

- How to go zero waste in the kitchen.
- How to go zero waste on packaging.
- How to stop using single-use items.
- How to re-hash and fix things.
- How to start growing your own food.
- How to save money by learning how not to buy.

Stop doubting it, your actions will influence the world. Help to spread the zero waste word and prove to the world that we can do it. We can fight climate change together, we can change our habits and achieve amazing results. Like the Swedes have. They are after all only people just like you and me. If they can WE can! We can reduce the US's landfill from 125 million tons to 2.5 million tons. With the average plastic item taking 350 years to break down and the population still on the rise, we are almost out of time.

We have to take action and start our zero waste life today. This book is here to help you take that step and make a that change that will save millions and make you a better, happier person. Jump in with me!

1 EAT MORE, THROW LESS: NO WASTE KITCHEN

The first and most obvious way to go zero waste in the household is in the kitchen. It is here in the kitchen that we fill the rubbish bin with packaging, leftovers and all manner of things. The kitchen is guilty for most of our household waste so let's attack it first. In this chapter I would like to give you some ideas about how to reduce your food waste and save some money in the process. Some people make money by exploiting the environment. Well, we're here to balance it out. What better way to make money than buying lovely fresh food, making healthy recipes and reducing your waste and your impact on the planet at the same time? Here's how I do it.

WHERE IS FOOD WASTED?

- Food is wasted in different parts of the production and consumption chain. How much is wasted in which step is dependent on where you live.
- Some food is sorted away and thrown because it's the wrong size or shape. Some of this food is saved and used for animal feed but most of it doesn't get used.
- Some food goes off during transport.
- Some food goes past its use-by date and is thrown away in the shop or at home (this generates a large amount of food waste from the home).
- Some food is cooked and then not eaten so it ends up being thrown away.
- Fruit and vegetables have the highest waste rate.
- Some estimates say that you could save up to 900 USD/year by wasting less food.

Here is a graph taken from an FAO (Food and Agriculture Organization of the United Nations) report showing how much food is wasted in the pre-consumption and post-consumption stages:
Per capita food losses and waste/year in different regions two text here.

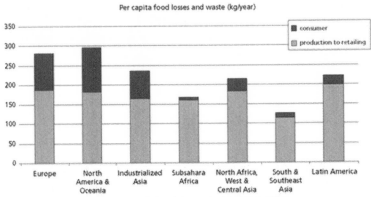

Source: Global Food Losses and Food Waste, Author: FAO, 2011

As you can see in the graph in Europe, North America, Oceania and industrialized Asia the food wasted by the consumer is approximately 40% of the total food waste. This is a huge amount! But it also gives us hope. It means that consumers like you and me can really make a difference simply by changing our habits and reducing our food waste.

Let us delve into what we can do to reduce this number..

SHOP FOR WHAT YOU NEED

The first step towards a zero waste kitchen is to start to keep track of what you've bought and used. Put a scrap of paper on the fridge and write a few basics on it that you know you eat regularly such as bread, milk, eggs, cheese. For a week keep a tally of how many loaves of bread or baguettes your household gets through, how many litres of milk you use per week or how much fruit you need. Next time you do your weekly shopping make sure you buy enough and not more than you used.

When you go grocery shopping take a 'shelfie' – a photo of your fridge and cupboards to remind you of what you have. Better to buy too little and have to make do without every now and again, than to waste your money on food you don't need. In fact, I found not having exactly what I need for the recipe makes the imagination juices flow and sometimes leads to a fantastic new creation!

Check the use-by dates of fresh food when you buy it. These are the dates to take notice of, rather than the best-before dates. Only buy what you can use before it expires (which is where step 1 comes into play). Be careful with fresh greens and spinach in a bag...don't fall for the 200g at 11 Euro/kg (or $/lb) trick if you know that you're the only one who likes it or if your recipe calls for only a handful of it. Most likely you'll use that handful and maybe one more and the rest will go off in the fridge. Pay 16 Euro/kg (or $/lb) for the 70g bag instead. We're talking a tiny difference in what you actually pay when you're buying such small amounts and it's just not worth the waste. Or have a bag of frozen spinach and only buy fresh when you're not planning on cooking it.

Make a list (more about that below).

HOW TO PLAN MEALS AND CREATE A SHOPPING LIST

It is impossible to make an accurate shopping list if you don't know what you're going to make in the coming week so meal planning is essential to zero waste. It does not need to be complicated. There are many resources and so much inspiration on the web. Use it, take it, steal it, copy paste it! I've tried so many that I couldn't tell you which one's which anymore. All of them have their pros and cons, and in the end none of them is really tailor made. You can definitely get a lot out of these apps and websites and who knows, maybe there's one out there now that would fulfill all your requirements. However as with most things, when you go past the beginner's phase you develop a more specific idea of what you want and you start to raise the bar.

For me, none of the digital aids I've tried has really cut it. So, I have my own system:

- Open a Word document and call it Meal Planning week X Month X.
- Check your fridge and cupboard and scour the web for recipes that include some of the ingredients you already have. Copy and paste the recipes and ingredients lists into your meal planning document. Don't worry about formatting yet.
- Check the portion sizes and decide how many portions you want to make. For example you may be 2 adults and one small child in the house and you want to have enough leftovers for lunch the next day so you need 5 portions.
- Calculate the portion factor: if the portion size in the recipe is 4 and you want 5 portions you divide your portions by the recipe's = 5/4 = 1.25. If you want less portions than the recipe's then divide the small number by the big number.
- Multiply (x) the ingredients by the portion factor to get the right

amount. Now edit all the amounts in your document e.g. 500g fish would become 500 x 1.25 = 625g.

- Now make your shopping list and make sure you include the amounts. If an ingredient appears in multiple recipes add the amounts and put the total on the list.
- Don't forget breakfast and snacks. Have some staple snacks and breakfasts and buy things you know you and your children like. Add these staples to the shopping list e.g. milk, bread, eggs, making sure you stick to the amounts you know you are going to eat. Actually I always buy extra bread and freeze it as we get through a lot of it in our family. This avoids further visits to the shops reducing the chances to buy stuff you don't need.
- Finally write on your documents what you are going to do with any leftovers that you are likely to have. Personally I recommend you leave a meal slot open and call it "leftovers" on day 3 of the week. The leftovers will likely build up so you have enough for a meal.

Don't plan for every day of the week as there are always days when you eat out or at somebody's house. 5 meals with enough for lunch and dinner usually works well for us.

If you do bigger batches to bulk cook be sure to freeze in reasonable portions which you know you will use up within one 24h period once defrosted. For this you need containers to freeze in! And since we don't want waste, this is one great way to re-use plastic packaging from your weekly shop. Just make sure you don't use glass as it can crack in the freezer.

One more word of advice: plan one super lazy meal each week. We all know that good intentions don't always win. Sometimes you're just too tired, come home too late or get sick. That's when it's time for pizza toast or pasta with tomato sauce and basil, or veggie burgers. Maybe you're an amazingly organized kitchen god/goddess and have a stash of home-made meals in the freezer from last week? Now's your moment to shine.

I've tried a myriad of apps and websites that do it for me and I'm never 100% happy with the results. I sometimes take whole meal plans from digital sources but I find copying and pasting everything into one document and doing my own shopping list with the right amounts is actually a more effective way of planning and reducing waste. I usually stick the whole thing on the fridge and make a note on the days when I have to put beans and pulses to soak, or I do them all at the weekend and then freeze them in portion sizes.

USE YOUR LEFTOVERS

No matter how good the meal plan was there will be leftovers. So why not accept it and plan for them? As I mentioned above, you can have a day a week where you eat leftovers. You can also have a few recipes in the bag for the usual suspects. Once this is in the system it'll be second nature. Here are some ideas but feel free to use those apps and websites you like best to find more ideas. The possibilities are endless!

Potato Patties
200g leftover mash (it can include other vege too)
a teaspoon of baking soda
2-3 tbsp of flour
1 egg
salt and pepper
a little bit of grated cheese, bits of leftover chicken, ham or just about anything salty

Mix it all together, make patties about 1 cm thick and fry them in a bit of oil. Sometimes I melt a slice of cheese on top, or poach an egg. Everybody loves these and as long as you have a bit of mash as the base you can mix most vegetables into this. You can grate carrots into it and courgettes too. This is great if you have children and need to disguise vegetables into food.

Make your own stock with trimmings
Have an ongoing bag in the freezer. Add all the trimmings from vege, fish bones, chicken bones, non-waxy cheese rinds, whatever really. When it's full, put it in a pot, add water and boil the heck out of it. Then sieve it, salt it and concentrate it by boiling even longer if you want to. It's a good idea to let meaty stocks cool down and then remove the fat if you're going to freeze for later, as fat doesn't keep well in the freezer. I usually make the stock when I'm planning on using it so I skip that step because the fat adds flavour to the dish and it's a pain in the backside to have an extra step.

Potato peel crisps
Wash your potatoes thoroughly before you peel them and save all the peels. Deep fry them, shake them in a bowl with a bit of kitchen roll under to get rid of some of the excess oil. Salt. Eat. Quick!

Vegetable and fruit over-night bread
25 g fresh yeast or 12.5g active dry yeast
500 ml cold water
600 ml strong flour

200 ml whole wheat or other wholegrain flour
2 tbsp oil
1 tsp salt
200ml leftover fruit or vege, grated

Mix the yeast with cold water in a large bowl. Add oil and salt. Add whole-grain flour. Add the rest of the flour. Mix. It should be like thick porridge. Not runny but not thick enough to knead. Add the fruit or vege. Add more flour if needed. These amounts can vary a little bit depending on the flour. Sprinkle a little flour on top and cover with a clean tea-towel. Put it in the fridge overnight (10-12 h).

The following morning, put a baking tray in the bottom of the oven and heat the oven up to 275°C.

Take the dough out of the fridge and place on a clean, floured surface. Roll into a sausage and cut the sausage into 10 pieces. Don't knead. Roll each piece up into a ball and flatten. Put them on a baking sheet or tray covered butter and breadcrumbs (to stop them from sticking). Place in the centre of the oven. Pour a glass of water into the tray that you left in the oven earlier. This will make them crunchy on the outside. Close the oven quickly so the steam doesn't escape. Bake for 10-12 minutes. Cool on the oven rack so they cool evenly.

Smoothies

I know this isn't the most original suggestion but please don't forget that brown piece of fruit that nobody fancies. Just squish it into a smoothy, add some berries or whatever else you have and whizz the heck out of it. Add water or juice to get the right texture for you and hey presto. You can also use smoothies as a way to add a bit of vege to your diet. Add frozen spinach or any other leafy green, avocadoes, cucumber...

Beans

Add leftover beans and lentils to salads, soups and tomatoey sauces.

Mash beans into patties and add any other bits and bobs, fry and enjoy.

THE POWER OF THE FREEZER

Take advantage of the technology in your home! Use your freezer to store batches of food for a later date. Remember to:

- Let foods cool down before you freeze them. Freezing food when hot will increase the temperature of the freezer and could cause other foods to start defrosting.
- Only refreeze food if you're cooking it in between. When food is thawed bacteria can multiply quickly, particularly at room

temperature. If you pop it in the freezer, the bacteria survive and are more likely to reach harmful levels on second thawing.

- A full freezer is cheaper to run as the cold air doesn't need to circulate so much, so less power is needed. Fill the freezer with everyday items you're bound to use, such as sliced bread or frozen peas.
- Avoid freezer-burn by wrapping foods properly.
- Freeze food in realistically sized portions. You don't want to have to defrost a stew big enough to feed eight when you're only feeding a family of three.
- Love your labels. It may seem a bother, but unless you label you might not remember what it is, let alone when it was frozen. You don't have to write an essay, just label the food clearly. Always add the date it was frozen.
- Defrosting is a must. An icy freezer is an inefficient one, so make sure you defrost your freezer if ice builds up. Don't worry about the food; most things will remain frozen in the fridge for a couple of hours while the freezer defrosts.

What not to freeze
Some ingredients don't survive the freezer so don't bother with those.

- Vegetables with a lot of water in such as courgettes, cucumber, raw peppers or lettuce go mushy in the freezer.
- Raw eggs crack. Boiled eggs turn rubbery.
- Soft herbs, like parsley, basil and chives are fine for cooking but they lose their texture in the freezer.
- Egg-based sauces, such as mayonnaise, will separate and curdle.
- Plain yoghurt, low-fat cream cheese, single cream and cottage cheese go watery.

COMPOSTING

There are inevitably parts of food that we can't eat. However many of these can be composted. You can compost in the garden, balcony or in the house, although I recommend the former two to avoid any bad smells and because it takes up precious space.

What can you compost?
- Fruit
- Vegetables
- Crushed egg-shells

- Garden plants
- Flowers
- Coffee grounds
- Newspaper and shredded paper
- Wood chips
- Make sure you have dry leaves and sticks together with food waste to balance out the carbon and nitrogen sources

What can't you compost?
- Meat
- Bones
- Fish
- Perennial weeds
- Diseased plants

How to do it
1. Dig a shallow hole and start there.
2. Put a compost container on top or build a box out of leftover wood.
3. Try to alternate dry and wet materials as you fill it.
4. Cover it and keep it a little moist, water during the dry season.
5. Turn the pile to get oxygen in

If you have your compost in the house, you can use any container as long as it has holes in it as you need oxygen. Make sure you add wet and dry materials so it doesn't get too soggy and start smelling. Turn it regularly. If you have a balcony keep it there so it's nice and airy.

LOVE YOUR PET

Did you know that the relationship between ancient wolf-dogs and our human ancestors was established thanks to rubbish? Let's get back to our roots then! It all started because people settled and became more abundant. Being as we are a dirty little bunch, the rubbish soon started to pile up. The delicious odour of half rotten dinners brought the wolves down from the hills to the human settlements and it was actually a lot easier to get food this way than through hunting. The naughty angry wolves got chased away by the humans but the nice ones were allowed to chomp on our garbage. This made for a much less smelly village, less rats and less diseases. The nicer the wolves were the more we became interested in them and soon we were using these hairy four-legged hounds for all sorts of things. Eventually, as usual with us sapiens, we claimed ownership over them and introduced them to our homes, and since then they've never left.

So, why spend a load of money on processed dog food when you have good quality, home-made dog food at your disposal already? Just make sure they get variety, avoid the no-nos (coming next) and have an emergency supply of dog food in case of left-over shortage. Our little sausage mongrel Peggy has some food issues after having started life as a wild street dog so she over-eats. As a result we have to be careful not to give her too much food but there's no reason not to freeze the leftovers for later use.

I have to be honest and say I'm no expert in cat diets or rabbits so I'm not going to tell you what to feed them. I believe rabbits don't eat animal products so if you're vegan this might be a good alternative. If you have a cat I'm sure you know better, but you probably also know that canned food isn't really their natural feed. Have a look at the content and see if you can use any of your leftovers to reduce your processed food consumption.

What your pet can't eat
There are some things that pets should definitely not eat.

- Chicken and poultry bones (but they can eat the cartilage).
- Fish bones.
- Avocado (concerns birds, horses, rabbits and ruminants)
- Alcohol
- Very salty things
- Chocolate
- Very sweet things
- Grapes and raisins (toxic)
- Milk and dairy in large amounts
- Nuts in large quantities
- Xylitol in large quantities
- Raw meat and eggs (for fear of Salmonella)

2 REUSE, RECYCLE: NO MORE PLASTIC PACKAGING

OK this topic is a whole book in its own right and it probably will be. There's so much to say about this and the need is so dire. We can't keep turning a blind eye and hoping that someone else will do something about it. Governments are finally starting to take action and you know how fast things happen in government (not!) so you understand that they must be scared to death to do something about the problem of plastic waste. Because it's such a huge topic and this is only a book to start you off on the right track, I'm going to give you some ideas that you can start with today, nothing complicated. Yes, you can do more, you can always do more, but start here and everything else will come of its own accord.

You may have noticed how much packaging supermarkets use nowadays. Some things need packaging to protect them in the fridge/freezer and some so that they will keep longer. But it's out of hand now. I recently saw a post on Facebook with a picture of a single, pre-peeled orange in a styrofoam dish, with paper wrapped around it and a layer of plastic on top. What?! An orange??? They keep for ages! They come ready-packaged in what we call peel!

When it comes to products, consumers have all the power. If nobody buys those oranges it's not good business for that shop to keep sourcing them. So, stop and think about whether there is any reason for the packaging. You may then say, but I was going to make duck a l'orange and these are the only oranges in the shop! I have to get them, I have no choice...REALLY? You have to have duck a l'orange tonight? Right now? You can't wait until another day when they have something more suitable? That sounds like the kind of behaviour I'm trying to curb in my 3 year old son. So don't be a 3 year old. If it's that important, go to another shop and buy oranges there instead. That way you are both removing your business from the shop that is providing an irresponsible product, and also gratefully giving your business to a shop that makes a more conscious choice. In this way we can wield our consumer power for the better. We choose what's in the shops not them. So make it a conscious choice and you will see that the face of your grocery store will slowly evolve to suit your needs.

Buying locally or at the market is also a good way to reduce packaging in general and even more so plastic. Usually if you go the local market things are on display and not wrapped up in packaging. Choose those products instead. Talk to the vendor as you buy and tell them you are trying to reduce packaging consumption. Can they wrap it in as little as possible? Feel the fruit and vege, smell it. Choose the ones that will be ready when you need them. You can talk to the vendor and ask for more information about each type of fruit. For example if you were going to make guacamole in 2 days they can help you choose avocadoes that will be ripe then, so that you don't get disappointed. I almost cry (yes I take food very seriously) if I open an avocado only to find that it's brown and full of fibers, or soft on one side and rock hard on the other. So spare your soul the damage and have a nice chat with your greengrocer.

BOTTLED WATER

OK I think if you buy this book you need to hear very little about bottled water. It's a well-known no-no if you're trying to change the world for the better. Millions of plastic bottles are binned daily. When we've become extinct our plastic waste will prevail for another 5 centuries. Imagine that. What a disgusting legacy. If you're not sure about the quality of your tap-water, just google it and you'll quickly find out if it's good to drink. There are places left even in countries that are considered to be modern, such as Flint in the US and Ibiza in Spain where you can't drink the tap-water. If you live or are visiting a place like this, there is no doubt you have to look after your health and buy clean water but even then you can limit the damage. Buy large water bottles and have a few small bottles at home/the hotel that you refill and have in the fridge or take with you. This will reduce the amount of plastic you're buying. Some places have water filling stations that you can take your bottles to refill them with clean water. Find out if there are any such places. It's much cheaper and you will cut down plastic drastically.

If you live in a place where the tap water is drinkable you can save a few pennies at the restaurant and ask specifically for tap water. If you're just out and about or at work, get yourself a nice metal bottle that you can have with you everywhere. They don't break and they last forever if you look after them. Just refill it and put it in your bag every morning before you leave. I know it sounds hard to remember but it's all about how much importance you give to it. If you really want to you will find a way to remember because you are a smart individual. Look, every day I have to prepare my three year old son's sandwich and water bottle and put it in his bag for school. I forget many, many things on a daily basis. So does my husband. We nag each other about all manner of small things. But never do we have to nag each other about Adam's snack box. Why? Because he is so important to us, we couldn't live with ourselves if it got to break time and he opened his bag to find it empty. If we forgot we would jump on our bicycle and cycle back from wherever to make sure he had something to eat and drink. It's amazing but so far we haven't forgotten a single time. Even the most forgetful person can introduce the bottle habit. You have to truly know that it's important to you first and then you'll find a system to remember to do it every day.

PLASTIC BAGS

There are a million ways to use less plastic bags. Your absolute number one strategy is to stop and ask yourself: Do I need this bag? I am an intelligent human being, I know stuff. I pride myself in being smart. Can I come up with a way to avoid using this bag? If not: Re-use it. Next time, get yourself a few shopping bags made out of other sturdier materials which you keep in your car or shopping trolley, take smaller nets or textile bags to put your fruit and vegetables in instead of using the ones they give you at the shop.
if you have a dog you'll know that plastic bags are almost inevitable in the city. Try to find a system to tie the bag so that you can re-open it. That way you won't use two bags if your dog does two number 2s. Use the same bag for both if possible.

When you buy bags you know you're going to throw away, such as doggy bags, think about what happens to them afterwards. Will they be incinerated? Then don't bother buying biodegradable, buy the thinnest smallest possible bag to reduce the amount of bi-products released on incineration and the energy and materials put into producing it. However if it's going to end-up in a land-fill, buy thin biodegradable bags instead if you must have a plastic bag. They still take forever to break down and some of them need specific conditions to which they will likely not be subjected at the landfill site. So do think again.

RE-USE PACKAGING

We've talked about plastic bags but there are other things you can re-use. Toilet roll and kitchen roll tubes can be used for fun artsy things with your children. They can be stuck to each-other, painted, cut, glittered and all sorts of shapes made out of them. I usually go on Pinterest and see what I can find. Recently I found a great project making Christmas glittery stars out of loo-roll tubes. It'll make you feel all rags-to-riches-ey using something so mundane to produce something so beautiful and the little ones will love it! Actually my little one is very happy running round tooting through empty toilet-roll tubes but it gets a bit much after a while so it's good to have alternatives. Be prepared to find glitter stuck to your face and in the corner of your eyes for the next year or so though. Think of it as a reminder of good times.

If you like a bit of gardening, re-use packaging such as egg-packs or anything that looks like a tray to sow seeds at the beginning of the season. They're the perfect size for a seedling. Sometimes you'll have to make small holes at the bottom with a pin so they can drain and that's it. You saved some pennies in plant pots and saved the world a little bit.

Tubs with lids such as yoghurt tubs can be used as tupperware.

Jars and glass bottles with a lid can also be re-used for food storage. I always have a jar available to make salad dressings with. You fill it with the dressing ingredients and shake it until they're fully blended. It makes a lovely well incorporated salad dressing or sauce.

FIREPLACE

If you have a fireplace I'm sure you won't be new to the idea of using paper, cardboard and tetra-paks as kindle. So really, this is just a reminder not to forget and to have a good place to keep your packaging bits. Of course this releases greenhouse gases, soot and other substances into the environment so burning is a last resort. At least this way you will generate heat for your home.

DIY

You'll notice in your new awareness of packaging that a lot of it comes from items such as sauces, dips, juices and pre-made foods. When you've decided to stop buying into the packaging industry these are possibly the hardest foods to let go of. I love hummus and pita bread, guacamole with nachos, fruit juices, mustard and ketchup on my burgers... but all of these items come in a plastic container or bag! But as my mum has said to me since I was a little girl, where there's a will there's a way. You bought this book because you know you have to find another way, right? Well here's my way: You can stop consuming some of these but what is common to all of them is that you can also make them yourself!

I don't believe in setting unreasonable expectations and there are many foods out there that we are so used to consuming that we don't understand anymore that they're made in a kitchen somewhere. The best way to do it is to pick a couple of those foods that you buy regularly and try to make them yourself. It takes a few attempts to perfect the flavour balance until it's right so you can't take on too many of these kitchen projects at once! So, let's get back to basics, and back to the kitchen. Here are a few things that are super easy to make and will save tonnes of packaging.

Hummus
    600g cooked chickpeas
    4 tbsp tahini (sesame seed) paste
    1-2 garlic cloves
    3-4 tbsp lemon juice
    100ml extra virgin olive oil
    1tsp of salt

Using a food processor or hand-held blender, add first the tahini and the lemon juice. Then add the water and oil and finally the chickpeas. Whizz to the desired consistency and taste. Add water, oil, salt or other spices e.g. paprika/parsley to taste.

Guacamole
    2-3 Avocados
    2 tbsp chopped fresh tomatoes
    1 tbsp chopped onions
    1 tbsp of lemon juice
    a sprinkle of chili powder or flakes (optional)
    1/2 tsp salt
    1 tbsp chopped cilantro
    a drizzle of olive oil

Mash the avocado with the back of a spoon. Add lemon juice and salt. Gently mix in the onions and tomatoes and sprinkle with the cilantro and chili flakes on top. Drizzle a little olive oil over it all.

Juice
Juice can be made out of most watery fruits. It's true that it requires a lot more effort than pouring juice from a tetra-pak so you won't drink juice quite as often. It will become a treat rather than an everyday routine. This may help you cut the amount of sugar in your diet. After all juice is not recommended as part of a healthy diet. We're supposed to eat the whole fruit so smoothies are a better and easier alternative if we still want to drink our fruit. That way you still get all the fibre and the feeling of fullness, as well as reducing the concentration of sugar in your drink.

If you have a juicer you can experiment with anything. If, like me, you only have a standard citrus juicer, use oranges, pomelo/grapefruit and lime as a base for your juices. Then with a blender make a smoothie with some other fruits. Filter using cheesecloth or a fine-mesh sieve or two layers of nylon tights. Add the filtrate to your citrus blend.

Oat Milk
  100g oats
  1-1.5L water
  1 pinch of salt
  1 pinch sugar

Blend the oats and 1L of water. Let the oats stew in the water for 30 minutes. Filter using cheesecloth or a fine-mesh sieve or two layers of nylon tights. Add a bit of salt and sugar to taste. Add more water if you want a thinner consistency.

Nut Milk
  150g nuts (e.g. almonds or cashews)
  1L water
  a pinch of salt

Roast the nuts lightly in a dry frying pan. Soak them overnight in water. Blend in a mixer or blender. Filter using cheesecloth or a fine-mesh sieve or two layers of nylon tights. Add a bit of salt to taste. If you find it too bland you can add sugar and/or vanilla powder or extract. Add more water if you want a thinner consistency.

3 SAY NO TO DISPOSABLE PRODUCTS (OR REUSE THEM)

GET YOUR PRINCIPLES CLEAR, AND STICK TO THEM

Backbone, find yours, suffer it, be proud of it and rejoice in the results. But make sure you know that sticking to your principles is not the easy way out. It's the only way out in this case though. It's hard work having principles, but start slowly and build that spine bone by bone and soon you'll have something sturdy to hold you up and weather you through the most powerful storms of marketing and plastic fantastic brain-washing.

ALTERNATIVES TO SINGLE-USE

Here are some things which exist in multiple-use version which you need buy only once. This will definitely save you some money and a lot of waste. Some of them require washing and drying. Try to air-dry where possible to reduce your energy consumption. Use only as much detergent as you need and no more. Buy eco-friendly detergent if you can. Even when you take into account the extra washing you will still be releasing less into the environment and consuming less resources than with single-use products. Stop buying paper and plastic kitchenware. It's never necessary as there are already plates, cups, glasses, knives and forks in your kitchen and at the restaurant. If any of these alternatives interest you I recommend having a look for them on Amazon. No point getting complicated! Amazon has most things and if you can't find it there please feel free to contact me. Of course depending on where you live they may or may not deliver but I'm sure you can quickly find your own options.

Rechargeable batteries
Yes, it might sound a bit old-school but we seem to have forgotten that rechargeable batteries exist. It's not as good as not using batteries at all but a much better alternative than throw away ones.

Paper tissues
Use a good old handkerchief instead and throw it in the wash when you're done.

Kitchen-roll
Use napkins for the table and a good quality dishcloth for the kitchen. You can even have on with you when you travel to avoid picking up unwanted paper towels at the restaurant.

Toilet paper
Eliminate or reduce toilet paper usage by using your bidet to have a wash after going to the toilet or by installing a toilet seat with a water stream. It's so much more hygienic than smearing it all around with dry paper. They even sell little showers that you can attach to your sink through a three-way valve and have hanging on a hook next to the toilet.

Plastic and paper straws
Use a steel straw or buy a cup with a built-in straw and lid.

Cling-film
Try finding a sandwich can or box to take to work or school. They also sell waxed fabric which you can use to cover things with instead of throw-away foil. You can also put a plate on top of the food if you only want to keep it in the fridge overnight. If you want to keep it in the fridge a bit longer, put it in glass containers with a lid. I often simply put the lid back on the pot I cooked it in and stick that in the fridge.

Drink cans and bottles
Single-serving drinks such as 33cl cans and bottles are also a big source of packaging. As always, awareness is key. What if you stopped drinking bottled beer and only ordered draught? Not hard is it. And if they don't have it, have a glass of wine or go somewhere else. Quit drinking fizzy drinks, they're terrible for you anyway, and if you do, go to McDonalds or Burger King and get them in a paper cup instead. Or get only fizzy drinks that come from a drinks tap not from a bottle or can.

Take-aways
Take-aways are a huge source of unwanted rubbish, the pizza box, the

salad plastic box and lid, the coffee cup, the sushi tray and lid and chopsticks with their paper cover. The truth is if you get a take-away you need something to take it away in. Invariably that means some kind of packaging. Maybe in future they will give it to you in glass tupperware for which you pay a deposit which you get back when you return it. Or they'll take a leaf out of Germany's book and have a system of returning mugs where you can return it to a different business and they all collaborate and use the same reusable cups.

That way you wouldn't have to depend on remembering to bring your own.

However, for the time being the only real solution is to avoid take-aways as much as possible, or bring your own food container. If you can enjoy your food at the restaurant then sit down and take a time-out to eat. If you can't then bring your own food as often as possible and think ahead. You know there are days when you can't cope with the thought of standing in the kitchen cooking. Have something in the freezer that you can just whip out and warm up in the oven or microwave on those occasions. Make sure you have a piece of fruit and water in your bag with you always so you're not completely desperate and have to stop for a quick fix.

Restaurants and cafés

Make a note of single-use items you end up consuming when you're out and about. At your favourite café, do they give you sugar in a sachet or is there a dispenser? Try asking them for a dispenser instead and explain your reasoning if possible. You never know, they might decide they want to change their ways and it may even be cheaper for them. If there are several places to choose from, maybe you could choose the ones who have the least wasteful policies. If you get offered a straw, which you often do when you have children with you, make sure to say a big fat NO. If it's self-service, don't take one. Ask for bottled ketchup or mayo instead of using sachets.

Nappies

If you have children you'll notice your single-use item usage increases drastically especially in the first few years. You quickly start to feel the impact you're having when you start producing bags full of nappies on an almost daily basis. Guess what? An alternative exists! They're made out of materials such as cotton and bamboo, and have an impermeable layer on the outside of what is commonly referred to as PUL. You can buy all-in-one nappies with both layers incorporated or you can buy muslin cloth (70cm x 90 cm or a bit bigger). Then you can buy PUL shells to go over the cloth. To learn how to fold the nappies go online and look on YouTube. There are many ways to fold these nappies so just try a few and choose the one that works best for you and your child. You will probably benefit from a few Snappys to keep the material in place. When the nappy gets dirty you rinse it in cold water if it's a number 2 and throw it into a breathable bag. You can place this bag in a metal bucket next to your changing station. Metal is better than plastic as it doesn't absorb smells. Wash everything at 40 to 50°C and do every three washes at 90 °C to get rid of any bacteria. Be careful with PUL as it doesn't wash at 90°C. This is why I prefer the separate layers. I can build the nappy up depending on how much absorbance is needed and wash the inner and outer layers separately. It's also by far the cheapest alternative. In order to comfortably survive you need three days' supply at about 8 per day that is 24 muslin cloths, 3 or 4 PUL layers and some extra layers such as small towels that you can fold into the nappy.

Breast pads for lactation
Similar to the all-in-one nappy construction, reusable lactation pads made out of similar materials are available. These are great. You just throw them in the wash and reuse. Make sure you have enough to cover you for a few days so you have time to wash and dry them.

Female sanitary articles
One of the downsides of the XX chromosome is that women are guilty for a lot of rubbish ending up in the system because of disposable sanitary products such as tampons and sanitary pads. There are amazingly comfortable non-disposable alternatives now. If you are used to tampons then I highly recommend you get yourself a silicone menstrual cup such as the Mooncup. It lasts forever and is used in a similar way to a tampon. If you prefer sanitary pads there are disposable ones that are made out of absorbent materials with an impermeable outer layer, similar to the breast pads and nappies mentioned above. These can be found on Amazon.

A little motivation
One of the issues I think we have to face in our generation is that the availability of single-use hygiene items has meant zero cleaning because we can just throw it away. People who have had it like this all their lives may not be used to coming into direct contact with dirt and bodily excretions. This produces a lot of resistance to change. It requires you to deal with the "disgust" factor. It's never going to be a pleasant experience cleaning poo or any other bodily fluid. It's a question of finding the motivation to start and then realising the benefits as you go along. Just like you wouldn't consider leaving your baby in a soiled nappy because the incentive to clean them is bigger than the disgust factor, you can also have the same attitude towards your own hygiene. We are after all choosing to make our children's and grandchildren's lives liveable, to avoid a war in the near future due to

lack of resources, and ultimately to save humankind from extinction. If we want the world to continue to be populated by the human species then we have no choice. It may seem like we do have a choice because single-use items are still available. However that's just a chimera set up by lazy politicians who work too slowly and are too interested in their own pockets as well as too scared of confronting the multi-million dollar industry that many people's fingers are in. There are strong forces working against banning these items and not everybody has the courage or know-how to stand up to them. We have to wage war on them guerrilla style, you and I, from our own turf. Nobody will do this for us. So I say, getting over the grossness of washing your own panty-liners (and I mean come one the washing machine does most of the job) is a small price to pay for the survival of future generations. Just as you got used to changing nappies and stopped (well almost) noticing the grossness, so will you get used to this.

4 FIX EVERYTHING (OR HAVE SOMEONE ELSE DO IT)

CLOTHES

There are a number of scenarios and a number of options when it comes to used up clothes.

Let's say your hem comes loose or you have a hole in your favourite trousers. The key word here is favourite of course. If you like the item and it's fixable then you can do it! So you put it into the fix pile and a year later there it is... yes I do know the feeling. The only way to fix this one is to understand what the problem is and address it. Are you afraid of picking up the sewing machine because it's been too long? Get an old kitchen towel and practice a bit on it first. The sewing machine's instructions will tell you everything you need to know and there's of course YouTube if you want to watch someone else do it first. Then go ahead and just do one trouser. It'll take an hour, yes, but how many hours of wear are you about to get out of those? And how long would it have taken you to actually replace the item? You would have most likely had to drive to a shop, search for the right thing, try it on, pay for it and drive back. Time consuming and expensive. Not to mention wasteful.

Here's how to hem trousers:
1. Open the old hem completely with a scalpel. Place it under the stitches and gently cut them loose. Remove the broken thread.
2. Try the trousers on with the shoes that you would normally wear with them so you can see how much you need to take them up.
3. Fold the trousers up with the fold on the underside to the right length. The trousers should be lightly touching your shoes.

4. Put some straight pins in them to keep the hem in place and walk around a little bit in front of a mirror. Are they the right length? Are your socks showing when you walk? Adjust the fold where necessary and pin it into place.

5. Take the trousers off and turn them carefully inside out making sure the pins stay in place. Now you can start sewing.

6. Measure the hem so that the fold on both sides is the same length and adjust it accordingly.

7. Iron the hem to make the folded edge sharp and straight.

8. Carefully try them on again to check they are still right.

9. If this is the first time the trousers are being hemmed and there is a lot of excess fabric, measure 3.8cm from the edge and make a line there with a ruler. Cut them excess fabric along the line. If you have pinking shears use them as they don't unravel the fabric.

10. Put the pins in at approximately 2.5 cm from the edge of the fabric.

11. Make a line with the chalk about 1.3cm from the hem (the part furthest from the edge of the fabric which marks the end of the trouser leg).

12. Take thread the same or as similar as possible in colour to the colour of your trousers. Sew making sure to only pick up a couple of stitches from the side that will be facing outwards. This will make the sewing almost invisible.

13. When you finish make a knot in the thread and then with the needle thread the end through a few stitches.

14. Try the trousers on again and check they are right. If not rip the stitches up and change the position of the sewing line and sew again.

If you hate sewing you can do the last steps using fabric tape as the glue between the fold. Just follow the instructions on the package.

If your item is so broken you don't know how to fix it, you don't have a sewing machine or you just can't do it, then pay for a seamster/seamstress to fix it. You will be so pleased, I promise. It's the most gratifying thing ever getting your old items back whole again.

When it comes to other items such as furniture and electronics it may require a bit more space to fix it. In some cases it requires a level of skill, or special tools, which we simply don't have. Sand-paper and a lick of paint can sort a lot out but if it's not that, find somebody in the area that fixes that kind of thing and take it there. Even if you then don't plan on keeping the item, you can sell it afterwards at a decent price on the second-hand market.

Which of course brings me to my next point. If you don't want the item because you don't like it, then fix it first and then sell it. It's never been easier to sell second-hand. Take a picture with your phone, load it onto Facebook's marketplace, Wallapop or any other second hand app. Write a short title and description. Spend no more than 5 minutes on each item and I promise you're going to manage to sell most of it. If you're feeling extra generous or nobody wants to buy the item then take it to the charity shop and somebody will sell it for you to a better home. You can have a charity basket or bag at home which you slowly fill and when it's full you take it to your local charity shop.

QUALITY VS PRICE

Often when we buy a new item we can't see the quality but we can see the price-tag. Cheap is very attractive but is it really better? Or cheaper really? My dad recently said to me "Nenita, after all these years I've finally realised that when it comes to tools, sometimes cheapest is not best. I've actually started to pay a bit more money to get better quality tools that don't break the first time I use them because you know what? It's actually cheaper than having to buy a new one." You can imagine my joy! Being as it is in our relationship I didn't start cheering and jumping up and down saying "I told you Dad! I've been telling you for yeeeeeears!!!" I controlled my impulse and instead quietly nodded, "Aha, well that's good". I didn't want him to get all defensive and never do anything like it again so I actually shut my mouth, for once. Anyway the point is that he IS right.

When I moved to Sweden where the weather wears down your soul (I recently left to somewhere a lot warmer) as well as your clothes, shoes, cars and skin I also learned to buy better quality stuff. So yes I did spend 150 Euros on my winter boots. But I still have them 10 years later and they are in mint condition. If I'd had 50 Euro ones I would have (a) lost my toes due to frostbite and (b) probably had to buy a pair every year or two, ending up in 5 or 6 pairs and a lot more money (and time) wasted. In fact, I bought a lovely pair of fashionable leather boots in Manchester with Mum for 50 pounds. I couldn't believe I'd found such a bargain. Guess what? I've had to have the zip changed 3 times on one boot and twice on the other. Yes. I still can't bear to throw them because I love them but hell, they are the most expensive boots I've ever bought! So try to identify which brands and materials last and buy better stuff when you need it. It's an investment and it will pay off.

Finally, if your items are so broken down that you can't sell them, fix them or give them away, re-cycle them. You can give textiles to H&M and they'll send them for recycling. You can also use them as cleaning rags at home. Look at the item and if any part of it can be recycled, take it to the recycling centre and they will help you dispose of it in a responsible way.

☐

5 GROW VEGETABLES AT HOME

A huge source of packaging is of course avoidable if you don't have to buy stuff. Packaging is there to keep things fresh and to protect them during transportation. If neither of these are required, then zut! you've eliminated a great deal of trouble for everyone. Apart from the waste created in the supermarket, there's also a lot of pesticide- and industrial fertilizer-waste which runs down into the soil upon watering or rain, and ends up in rivers, lakes and seas. The effects of these are often, needless to say, not great, as they disturb the natural balance of living ecosystems. Even if they are not directly poisonous (which many are) they may cause overgrowth of something which can then not be consumed at the same pace and ends up clogging water pools or feeding parasites instead.

Growing your own vegetables has many other effects on you and your immediate surroundings. It keeps you out of the house for a while, making sure you get fresh-air and maybe a bit of sunshine (depending on where you live). It allows you to experience the sensations and smells that the earth and plants have to offer, which I believe has a positive effect on people's emotional state. Maybe we have some ancient instinct that associates these smells and sensations with food and water. Then there's the results of your hard labour which will be a healthier body and mind and fantastic, super tasty food which you will not regret having put time and effort into.

GARDEN OR ALLOTMENT

Some housing associations offer the possibility of renting a little allotment and there are plenty of allotment schemes around in towns and cities. Find out about what's available in your area. Make sure it's close - walking distance. Life's busy enough and the point isn't to have yet another thing hanging over you that you feel guilty about. It's about doing something for yourself, your health and the environment, and enjoying the process as well as the results. If you have a garden then you are a lucky devil, so use it. This is not a book about gardening and there are many books written about the topic which I'm sure you will read if you decide to do this. This book is about ideas, understanding that they are do-able and giving you a little push in the right direction so you know what the next step is.

My recommendation is to buy a short simple book on the topic of growing a vegetable patch. They will take you through the necessary steps. Some vegetables are picky and some are easy. Please, start easy! Try a couple of varieties of potatoes, some onions, some courgettes and maybe some green-beans the first year. That will prepare you and your soil. You can add a little herb garden and a few salad leaves to give variety. All of those are fairly easy. Fruit and berry trees and bushes, large vegetables like pumpkins and melons, and delicate things like strawberries can wait until next year. Tomatoes are also a good one but they require a little care. It takes a few years to learn what to do and what not to in that particular patch of soil. The longer you have your vegetable garden the easier it gets. You do however have to make sure that you put the essential nutrients back into the soil so that it keeps producing quality crops. You also have to make sure you rotate your vegetables to balance out the nutrient uptake from the soil and to reduce the incidence of disease in your plants.

Most of the back-breaking work comes at the beginning, in the spring, when the soil needs working. After that it's mostly maintenance. You have to be able to access your vegetable garden every day or every other day during the warmest part of the year. During late spring and summer, weeds grow fast so it's best to do a bit of weeding every day and some watering. If you can set up a watering station or some kind of irrigation system you will save yourself a lot of work and get better produce. Make sure if you go on holidays in the summer, that you have somebody that can come and water your plants. Otherwise you are wasting your time digging and sowing. By removing weeds and the natural inhabitants of that soil, you're also stripping it of its ability to keep nutrients and water. We often want to then grow plants that are not naturally occurring and most likely require more regular watering than the occasional rainfall, and the addition of nutrients to the soil.

One way to reduce the work that growing your own food requires is of course to grow crops that are naturally occurring in that climate. Then you only have to maintain them, water and weed during extreme weather conditions, check for parasites, and of course harvest the produce. The rest of the time they will be ok without much help. Personally, I'm very interested in this way of growing food. Perennial plants (plants that live for several years) will also make your garden easier to maintain as you won't have to churn the soil and sow seeds every spring.

Here's an idea of what lies ahead if you decide to take on this project:

Spring
Dig up the patch and remove grass and plants, including the roots. You'll have to invest in some tools for this. Check your local second-hand store to see what you can find!

Once everything is removed, you will have to add a bit of manure and mix it with some compost. Leave it for a few days and plan your garden.

Plan when to sow what and where. Make sure you divide the plants into groups because they will need crop rotation. You can find a lot of information out there about this. Plants that are closely related should not be grown in the same place year after year as they are likely to infect each other with diseases. Therefore most gardeners rotate between 3-4 patches and divide their plants into groups so as to avoid planting similar ones two years in a row on the same patch. belonging to 4 different groups and each year you have to plant them in a different patch so you rotate between 4 patches. For example group 1 could be tomatoes/potatoes, group 2 brassicas (kale/cabbage/broccoli) group 3 roots (parsnip/carrot) and onions and group 4 legumes (beans).

Make lines and divide your garden according to your plan and your groups and start sowing. If you live in a colder climate, sow your seeds indoors in egg-cartons and keep them moist. Then when they start growing transfer to a larger pot. Finally, when you are sure that the temperature will not dip under freezing point, plant them in your garden. It's good if you can harden them by having them outside during the day for a week or so, and taking them in at night. Take into account that you will need quite a lot of space to keep these little egg-cartons and plant pots, so clear some tops and reserve them for your little green babies.

Some plants require even warmer soil. For example, beans require a soil temperature of about 15°C so they will have to stay in for a little longer. Like I said all this information is available in a proper gardening book. This is just so you get an idea of whether it's something you want to do.

When you sow your seeds outside or when you first plant the seedlings, keep the soil moist and protect them from the harsh sun and from predators by covering them with white garden fabric.

Summer
Remove the garden fabric. Weed a little every day, carefully so you don't destroy your plant's roots. Be sure to check for parasites and remove them when necessary.

Water your plants every day to every other day when the rainfall is low. Even if it's rained a bit it has to rain quite a lot for it to penetrate the soil.

Also try to do the watering when the sun is low, in the morning or evening. Otherwise a considerable amount will evaporate before getting to the roots. Also you have to water the soil, not the leaves. It's important for nutrient transport up the plant that the leaves are not excessively wet. Evaporation through the leaves pulls the liquid sap up the plant and allows the roots to suck more nutrients up.

When fruits come out cover them with netting so the birds don't get to them before you do. By now you will start to harvest early crops, such as sugar snap peas, summer carrots, courgettes and potatoes. Where you've harvested and the plants have given all their produce, you can sow new fast-growing varieties of plants. Beans are good, salad leaves, mangold and little spring onions.

Autumn

Continue to harvest into the autumn. When your plants have given you all they've got (late autumn) cut them down and add the leaves to the compost or spread big leaves over the soil. If you have berry bushes and fruit trees now's the time to do some pruning. Do a final weeding session and turn the soil. Cover the soil with big leaves or fabric to protect the nutrients from disappearing and protect from frost. Some bulbs can also be planted now so that they come up in early spring.

Leave it to rest until spring!

GROWING VEGETABLES AND HERBS ON YOUR BALCONY

If you don't have a patch of soil outside there's a lot you can do on a balcony. You can buy potato grow bags and have them out there. You can use big plant-pots to grow tomatoes, peppers and cucumbers in. Some of these plants are very decorative too. And of course you can have all manner of herbs in smaller pots, as well as salad leaves.

Some vegetables want to spread sideways quite a lot. Courgettes, melons and pumpkins tend to want to grow out so if you don't have the space these are not great for a balcony.

Be sure to renew the soil in the pots every year to stop diseases from spreading. Also remember that most balconies are protected from the rain. In addition the area of soil available to the plants is relatively little compared to of they were planted outside so balcony plants require more regular watering.

GROWING VEGETABLES AND HERBS INDOORS

Even if you don't have a balcony you can still grow herbs on the windowsill and even small varieties of tomatoes and chilli-peppers. Just choose small ones and be selective- you only have enough space for your very favourites. Growing indoors is a little different because it gets warmer and drier so make sure you air the room and water them enough but not too much. Water-logging is a big cause of indoor plants perishing.

Some people love growing their own plants so much that even without a balcony they can still produce fruit and vege by using hydroponics or buying an indoor greenhouse. In fact, my brother-in-law is an avid indoor gardener and he produces fantastic and very varies chili peppers and tomatoes using these methods. This is unfortunately not my area of expertise so I do not wish to delve deep into the topic in this book. I just wanted to mention it because it's worth having a look at if you can't grow anywhere but indoors.

6 LESS IS MORE: BUY LESS AND BE MORE

Buying less will most definitely save you money, lots of money, whilst filling up your self-esteem bank and your feel-good bank and having a real effect on our future survival and well-being. There are many posts out there giving advice on how to get better deals and spend less money. Sure, getting more for your money isn't a bad thing. Let's get one thing straight here: we are coming from a different angle. We're not aiming at spending less money or getting more for your money. That is a pleasant side-effect of your new minimalist lifestyle. Saving money according to many, involves buying larger quantities for less money per unit or per kg/lb. Does this attitude really lead to less consumption? You guessed it. The answer is no, quite the opposite. It leads to more not less consumption. You'll spend the same or slightly less per cup if you have 1kg of coffee at home as opposed to a little 250g bag. But you will likely also have that extra cup when you feel like it, because hey, don't worry, there's a ton of coffee left. If you have a never-ending roll of kitchen paper you'll find yourself drying the table with it when you would normally have used a cloth. If you buy two for one bars of chocolate, you'll eat two bars of chocolate instead of one! Trust me on this one, it's false economy and it's one of the pillars of consumerism. Supermarkets aren't being nice when they do 2 for 1 deals. They know full well what they're doing and that in the end it's going to benefit them, not you. SO let's get our socks on straight - we want less items entering our home, not cheaper ones.

HOW TO BUY LESS

My number one most effective strategy is this: walk away. If you do nothing else in this whole book, please do this. Just learn to take a deep breath, be mindful of the impulsive character of your brain and walk away from the neon lights or the beautiful blouse or the fantastic special offer. Do the rest of your errands first while you think about it. And while you are thinking about it, think about why you want that, how you will use it, how much you need it or not. If you feel like you need it (note I didn't use want) consider first if you can make do for a little bit longer without it. If this is an impossibility and you still have the energy to go back to the shop then go ahead, buy it. For me this is what it's all about, this change in attitude towards buying and owning items. Every time I go home without the purchase I celebrate in my heart that little win. Of course, it also leaves me with a bit more money to do something special with or simply to invest in my sons' future.

Buying something new gives a little bit of a rush at the time because we love beauty and we have fantastic imagination and can picture ourselves in our perfect world getting much enjoyment out of this lovely new thing. Sadly, the feeling is soon forgotten so it must be repeated in order to re-live it. However not buying gives a different more permanent feeling of well-being, of doing the right thing for yourself and everybody around you. It makes you feel like you are the kind of person who can think, who can control the crazy monkey brain, who has principles and sticks to them. It builds strength, confidence and character. You get to know yourself, your needs, your longings and to understand which needs are real and which ones are just that region of the brain that lights up when tricked by the flashy neon marketing tricks that so many employ. This feeling of control, calm and understanding of the bigger picture, unlike the small buying rush, stays with you, moving you forwards to continue to build your character and thus changing the course of life. That is a permanent effect and it makes you feel proud. It's the ultimate kick. It's finding the strength to change what can be changed, to the better. I can recommend it.

The Bullshit Detector: questions to ask yourself before buying
- Am I replacing something that I had to get rid of or am I buying something new?
- Why do I need this now when I didn't need it before?
- Has something changed in my life that means I need this?
- How will this solve a problem in my life?
- Can I solve the problem any other way?
- Can I borrow something like this from somebody?
- Can I find it second-hand?
- Am I buying this because I'm lazy?
- Are there other options that require less buying?

If it's an item of clothing:

- Is the style of this item something that will stand the storms of fashion for years to come?
- How often do I think I will wear it?

If it's entertainment/hobbies:
- Do I have time to use this every week or at least every two weeks?
- Will this bring me rest?
- Will this re-charge my batteries somehow?
- Will it bring me health benefits?
- Can I achieve any of this in a different way?
- Am I being lazy?

A good example would be buying an indoor bicycle instead of going out running when you already have a pair of running shoes and you live in a place with decent weather. You think that buying, the rush of it, the novelty of it, will make you stick to your plan. However you haven't managed to get your bum out of the door a single time to go running. So how long do you really think the novelty will last? Why is an indoor bike so much better than going running? It's not really, is it? Why is running hard? Will the same things be difficult about biking? Try to understand the underlying reason why you didn't go running and see if this may carry-over to the biking project. Do you have an injury that means you can't run but biking is feasible? Well in that case maybe you're onto something. Do you bike in the summer but not in the winter because of the weather? Then maybe an indoor bike would work for you.

MAKING A BUDGET

Awareness is key when you're trying to make a change. Creating a budget is something that most people know they should do, but very few actually get round to it. I can tell you if you've never had a budget you're in for a treat. Your budget will tell you what to do when you're having an internal fight about whether or whether not to buy. It's like making yourself a spending compass that you can follow when you're feeling lost. Doing the budget means you've already made a decision as to how much you're willing to spend on what. In doing so you have to decide what's important to you and what isn't. What are you prepared to spend your hard earned cash on? How much? And what is need and what is luxury? In other words, what are your priorities? And above all how much money will you have left if you stick to the budget and what are you going to do with it?

The essential first step in creating a budget is book-keeping. Nowadays it's much easier than before thanks to modern technology. You need to do some book-keeping in order to understand what you usually do with your money, and identify where to reduce your spending and by how much. Here's how to do it:

Go in to your internet bank at the end of the month. Download your bank statement and go through it.

Based on what you can see create an Excel sheet with the necessary headings e.g. car, groceries, eating and drinking out, bills and insurances, rent/mortgage/interest and so on.

Fill them in. Some banks will allow you to export to excel so you can copy and paste the amounts into each column and add them up at the end.

Do the book-keeping for a few months before you decide on your budget.

Creating your budget in 4 simple steps

1. Look now at the figures you've come up with and decide which areas you would like to improve upon. What are essential spendings and which ones are more impulsive?

2. Make realistic spending goals for each of the headings. Some expenses never change. Some you can control. Try to cut down your spending by 10% in a few chosen areas to begin with. Don't be too harsh on yourself just yet. Otherwise you may end up not being able to live up to your expectations and blowing the whole project.

3. How much would that leave you with at the end of the month? If you do this for a year or 2 years, how much money will you have then? What will you do with the money? Maybe reduce your interest payments by paying back your loans faster? How much money would that allow you to save up or use when you have paid the loan? Investing the money in order to generate more money and retire 5 years earlier? Paying for your children's education or hobbies? Going on that dream holiday? Cutting down your working hours? You name it.

4. Now for the action plan. Everything before this has been about building an awareness and setting realistic goals. Now you're going to achieve them. What exactly are you going to do in order to reduce your expenditure by the amount you have set? You could for example not buy new clothes, only second-hand. You could include all your leftovers in your meal-plan and buy a little less meat this month. Quit drinking beer every day and save it for the weekends only. Go out and eat one less time a week. These are small changes but the results are cumulative and they will be BIG bucks in the end!

Now go ahead and get rich!

OTHER WAYS TO STOP YOURSELF FROM OVER-BUYING
- Have a list when you go to the shops.
- Limit the time you're allowed to shop.
- Don't window shop.
- Leave you card at home and take cash - this is a method that works for many people. It's harder to give your cash away because it's a physical thing. Also you can only spend what you've got and if there are a number of things on the list you can't just go crazy.□

CONCLUSION

I hope that this book has given you the tools you need and some extra motivation to start you on your zero waste home and lifestyle. It's no easy feat and it's a change that you make slowly over time. Pick a few key areas to work on first and when you're comfortable take on a few more. I started out increasing my recycling capabilities. Then I went on to meal planning and left-over management. Then I started growing my own food and so on and so forth. I'm still working on it and I'm definitely not at zero waste yet. However I have improved greatly, my awareness is thousands of percents broader than a few years ago and I hope that by writing this book and you reading it, I'm taking yet another step in reducing waste, now through my readers' efforts. Thank you so much for jumping over to the zero waste side. You are building a better future for all of us.

ONE LAST THING...

If you enjoyed this book or found it useful I'd be very grateful if you'd post a short review on Amazon. Your support really does make a difference and I read all the reviews personally so I can get your feedback and make this book even better. The better the book, the more people will read it and start their own journey to their Zero Waste Home.

You can also help spread the word by posting your success stories and recommending well sourced information to people.

If you would like to contact me after reading this book, please do so through my publisher's Facebook page:

https://www.facebook.com/Tropical-Publishing-Group